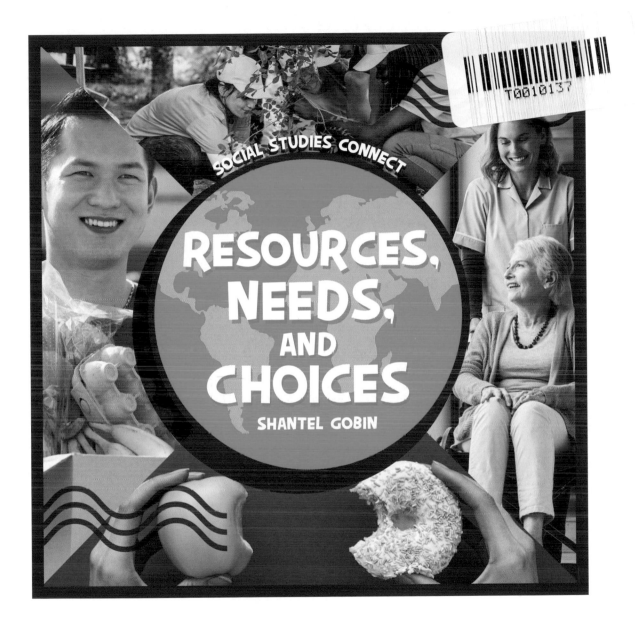

SOCIAL STUDIES CONNECT

RESOURCES, NEEDS, AND CHOICES

SHANTEL GOBIN

Rourke™

BEFORE AND DURING READING ACTIVITIES

Before Reading: *Building Background Knowledge and Vocabulary*

Building background knowledge can help children process new information and build upon what they already know. Before reading a book, it is important to tap into what children already know about the topic. This will help them develop their vocabulary and increase their reading comprehension.

Questions and Activities to Build Background Knowledge:

1. Look at the front cover of the book and read the title. What do you think this book will be about?
2. What do you already know about this topic?
3. Take a book walk and skim the pages. Look at the table of contents, photographs, captions, and bold words. Did these text features give you any information or predictions about what you will read in this book?

Vocabulary: *Vocabulary Is Key to Reading Comprehension*

Use the following directions to prompt a conversation about each word.
- Read the vocabulary words.
- What comes to mind when you see each word?
- What do you think each word means?

Vocabulary Words:
- employees
- resources
- shelter
- volunteer

During Reading: *Reading for Meaning and Understanding*

To achieve deep comprehension of a book, children are encouraged to use close reading strategies. During reading, it is important to have children stop and make connections. These connections result in deeper analysis and understanding of a book.

Close Reading a Text

During reading, have children stop and talk about the following:
- Any confusing parts
- Any unknown words
- Text to text, text to self, text to world connections
- The main idea in each chapter or heading

Encourage children to use context clues to determine the meaning of any unknown words. These strategies will help children learn to analyze the text more thoroughly as they read.

When you are finished reading this book, turn to the last page for **After-Reading** activities.

TABLE OF CONTENTS

EVERYONE, EVERYWHERE

It doesn't matter who you are.
It doesn't matter where you live.

Every person on the planet has needs.

A NEED INDEED

Everyone needs air, food, and water.

DID YOU KNOW?

The human body is made up of about 60% water. No wonder we can't live without it!

Everyone needs sleep, clothes, and **shelter**.

Everyone needs to learn and to love.

There are so many ways to show love. One way is to **volunteer**. Kids, just like you, can help build homes for others!

MEETING OUR NEEDS

The world is filled with **resources** to meet our needs.

Many come from the earth itself.

Tantalum is a natural resource. It is found in the Democratic Republic of Congo, Africa. Without it, there would be no cell phones!

We can buy the things we need.

We can also trade.

We need each other to make the world work. Can you say people power?

DID YOU KNOW?

The Golden Temple in India has more than 10,000 employees. They feed 100,000 people for free each day!

CHOICES, CHOICES, CHOICES

There are many different ways we can fulfill our needs.

Sometimes we have to make choices.

Sometimes, we can meet a need and do something we enjoy at the same time.

DID YOU KNOW?

There are many jobs where people get to do something they love while helping others.

PHOTO GLOSSARY

employees (em-PLOI-eez): people who are paid to work for another person or a business

resources (REE-sors-ez): things that are of value or use

shelter (SHEL-tur): a place that offers protection from bad weather or danger

volunteer (vah-luhn-TEER): to offer to do a job without pay

ACTIVITY

MY NEEDS

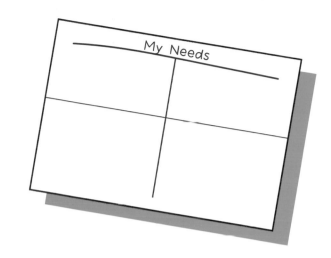

Supplies

paper   crayons
ruler

Directions

1. Using the ruler, draw a line down the middle of your paper, vertically.
2. Using the ruler, draw a line across the middle of your paper, horizontally.
3. Draw a picture of something you need in each box.
4. Label each picture with a word.
5. Ask a friend or family member to do this activity too.

Share your drawings. Did you draw the same things? Did you draw different things? Were some of your needs also things that you enjoy?

INDEX

ABOUT THE AUTHOR

Shantel Gobin is an urban educator. She enjoys living in Brooklyn, New York, with her family. She loves to volunteer and help others in need.

AFTER-READING ACTIVITY

With a parent, go online and do some research. Explore ways to volunteer in your community. How could you help people get what they need? Discuss your research with a family member an maybe even become a volunteer!

Library of Congress PCN Data

Resources, Needs, and Choices / Shantel Gobin
(Social Studies Connect)
ISBN 978-1-73165-637-7 (hard cover)(alk. paper)
ISBN 978-1-73165-610-0 (soft cover)
ISBN 978-1-73165-619-3 (eBook)
ISBN 978-1-73165-628-5 (ePub)
Library of Congress Control Number: 2022943027

Rourke Educational Media
Printed in the United States of America
01-0372311937

© 2023 Rourke Educational Media

www.rourkebooks.com

Edited by: Catherine Malaski
Cover design by: Morgan Burnside
Interior design by: Morgan Burnside
Photo Credits: Cover, page 1: ©goc/ Getty Images, ©South_agency/ Getty Images, ©Dean Mitchell/ Getty Images, ©dima_sidelnikov/ Getty Images; page 4: ©xuanhuongho/ Shutterstock.com; page 5: ©SewCream/ Shutterstock.com, ©I'm Conqueror/ Shutterstock.com; pages 6-7: ©Monkey Business Images/ Shutterstock.com, page 7: ©hadynyah/ Getty Images; page 8: ©Kenishirotie/ Getty Images; page 9: ©PixelCatchers/ Getty Images; page 10: ©Rawpixel.com/ Shutterstock.com; page 11: ©oes/ Shutterstock.com, ©Kyle M Price/ Shutterstock.com; page 12: ©Ingus Kruklitis/ Shutterstock.com; pag 13: ©Maksim Safaniuk/ Shutterstock.com, ©Tatiana53/ Shutterstock.com; page 14: ©JackF/ Getty Ima page 15: ©Lisa F. Young/ Shutterstock.com; pages 16-17: ©PRABHAS ROY/ Shutterstock.com; page ©PeterHermesFurian/ Getty Images, ©Xantana/ Getty Images; pages 18-19: ©Mukhina1/ Getty Images page 19: ©Ellona Kritskaya/ Shutterstock.com; pages 20-21: ©FatCamera/ Getty Images; page 21: ©L Business/ Shutterstock.com, ©Mlenny/ Getty Images; page 22: ©jacoblund/ Getty Images, ©Riccardo Mayer/ Shutterstock.com, ©Chadolfski/ Shutterstock.com, ©AaronAmat/ Getty Images